Sex

The Art of Mastering Intimacy

By
Davis Williams

All rights reserved. No part of this publication may be reproduced, distributed, or transmitted in any form or by any means, including photocopying, recording, or other electronic or mechanical methods, without the prior written permission of the publisher, except in the case of brief quotations embodied in critical reviews and certain other noncommercial uses permitted by copyright law.

Copyright © Davis Williams, 2023.

Table of content

Chapter 1: Understanding sexual anatomy and physiology

Chapter 2: Building trust and communication in sexual relationships

Chapter 3: Navigating consent and boundaries in sexual experiences

Chapter 4: Exploring sexual desires and preferences

Chapter 5: Enhancing sexual pleasure and satisfaction

Chapter 6: Managing and overcoming sexual difficulties and dysfunctions

Chapter 7: Understanding and addressing sexual trauma and abuse

Chapter 8: Building intimacy and connection in sexual relationships

Chapter 9: Navigating different sexual orientations and identities

Chapter 10: Developing a positive and healthy self-image when it comes to sexuality

Chapter 11: Understanding and managing the impact of past experiences on current sexual relationships

Chapter 12: Practical tips and exercises for mastering intimacy in sexual experiences

Chapter 1: **Understanding sexual anatomy and physiology**

Sexual anatomy and physiology is a complex and multifaceted subject that involves many different body systems and structures. Understanding this topic can help individuals make informed decisions about their sexual health and pleasure.

The anatomy of the male and female reproductive systems plays a crucial role in sexual activity and fertility. The male reproductive system consists of the testes, which produce sperm, and the penis, which is used for intercourse. The female reproductive system includes the ovaries, which produce eggs, the uterus, which holds a developing fetus, and the vagina, which is the canal through which sperm travels to reach the egg.

In both males and females, sexual arousal is driven by the release of hormones and increased blood flow to the genital area. During intercourse, stimulation of the genital area can lead to orgasm, which is the peak of sexual pleasure. Orgasm is a complex physical and psychological process that involves the release of various hormones and neurotransmitters.

It's important to note that sexual anatomy and physiology can vary greatly from person to person. Factors such as age, genetics, and overall health can all impact sexual anatomy and function. Additionally, some individuals may experience sexual dysfunctions, such as difficulty achieving orgasm, which can be addressed with medical treatment.

In conclusion, understanding sexual anatomy and physiology is essential for making informed decisions about sexual health and pleasure. It's important to remember that everyone's experiences are unique and that it's normal for sexual anatomy and function to change over time.

If you have concerns or questions about your sexual health, it's best to consult a doctor or sexual health specialist

Chapter 2: **Building trust and communication in sexual relationships**

Building trust and communication in sexual relationships is crucial for creating a healthy and satisfying intimate life. Trust and communication help partners feel safe and connected, and allow them to freely express their desires and boundaries.

Trust is essential in sexual relationships as it creates a sense of safety and security, allowing partners to be vulnerable and open with one another. Trust is built over time through consistent and honest communication, transparency in decision-making, and respect for boundaries.

Effective communication is key to building trust and creating a healthy sexual relationship. It's important to regularly check in with your partner to ensure that both partners feel comfortable and respected. This includes discussing desires, boundaries, and any potential concerns or fears. Communication also involves actively listening and being present in the moment during intimate experiences.

It's important to remember that communication is a two-way street, and both partners should feel comfortable expressing their thoughts and feelings. In some cases, one partner may be more reserved or less comfortable with expressing themselves, in which case it may be helpful to seek out therapy or counseling to work through these challenges.

It's also important to discuss and negotiate consent in sexual relationships. Consent is a mutual agreement between partners to engage in sexual activity, and it is crucial for maintaining respect and safety in intimate relationships.

In conclusion, building trust and communication in sexual relationships is essential for creating a healthy and satisfying intimate life. Regular check-ins, effective communication, and open and honest discussions can help build trust and ensure that both partners feel comfortable and respected. If you have concerns or challenges in your sexual relationship, it's important to seek out help and support.

Chapter 3: **Navigating consent and boundaries in sexual experiences**

Navigating consent and boundaries in sexual experiences is essential for creating a safe and respectful intimate environment. Consent and boundaries help ensure that all partners are comfortable and engaged in sexual experiences on their own terms.

Consent is a mutual agreement between partners to engage in sexual activity, and it is crucial for maintaining respect and safety in intimate relationships. Consent can be given verbally or non-verbally, but it should always be clear and enthusiastic. It's important to note that consent can be withdrawn at any time, and it's essential to respect your partner's boundaries.

Setting and communicating boundaries is also a key aspect of navigating consent in sexual experiences. Boundaries can encompass a wide range of topics, including what types of sexual activities are acceptable, preferred levels of physical intimacy, and preferred frequency of sexual experiences. It's important for partners to regularly check in with each other to ensure that both partners feel comfortable and respected.

In some cases, one partner may struggle to communicate their boundaries, in which case it may be helpful to seek out therapy or counseling to work through these challenges. Additionally, it's important to remember that boundaries can change over time, and it's essential to continue checking in with each other and being open to making changes as needed.

It's also important to be aware of the potential for power imbalances in sexual relationships, such as those based on factors such as age, gender, or social status. In these cases, it's crucial to ensure that all partners have equal agency and are able to freely give and withdraw consent.

In conclusion, navigating consent and boundaries in sexual experiences is essential for creating a safe and respectful intimate environment. Regular check-ins, clear and open communication, and a commitment to respecting boundaries and consent can help ensure that all partners feel comfortable and engaged in sexual experiences on their own terms.

Chapter 4: **Exploring sexual desires and preferences**

Exploring sexual desires and preferences is a crucial aspect of creating a fulfilling and satisfying intimate life. Understanding and communicating your own sexual desires and preferences, as well as those of your partner, can help you build a stronger and more connected relationship.

It's important to remember that everyone's sexual desires and preferences are unique, and there is no right or wrong way to experience or express sexual desire. Some people may be more comfortable exploring and communicating their desires, while others may struggle with these conversations.

To explore your own sexual desires and preferences, it's essential to take the time to reflect and self-explore. This may involve engaging in solo sexual activities, reading books or articles about sexual health, or seeking out therapy or counseling to work through any challenges.

Once you have a better understanding of your own desires and preferences, it's important to communicate them to your partner. Communication is a key aspect of exploring and understanding sexual desires and preferences, and it's essential to create a safe and supportive environment where both partners feel comfortable discussing these topics.

It's also important to respect your partner's desires and preferences, even if they are different from your own. Finding ways to accommodate and support each other can help build a stronger and more connected relationship.

In some cases, partners may struggle to find common ground in terms of sexual desires and preferences, in which case it may be helpful to seek out therapy or counseling to work through these challenges. Additionally, it's important to remember that desires and preferences can change over time, and it's essential to continue checking in with each other and being open to making changes as needed.

In conclusion, exploring sexual desires and preferences is a crucial aspect of creating a fulfilling and satisfying intimate life. Regular check-ins, open and honest communication, and a commitment to respecting each other's desires and preferences can help you build a stronger and more connected relationship.

Chapter 5: **Enhancing sexual pleasure and satisfaction**

Enhancing sexual pleasure and satisfaction is a crucial aspect of creating a fulfilling and satisfying intimate life. Whether you are in a committed relationship or exploring your sexuality, taking steps to increase your sexual pleasure and satisfaction can help you feel more confident and connected to your partner.

There are a number of strategies you can use to enhance sexual pleasure and satisfaction, including exploring new sexual techniques and activities, using sex toys and other sexual aids, and seeking out therapy or counseling to address any challenges that may be impacting your sexual experiences.

One important aspect of enhancing sexual pleasure and satisfaction is communication. It's essential to have open and honest conversations with your partner about your sexual desires and preferences, as well as any challenges you may be facing. This can help build trust and create a safe and supportive environment where both partners feel comfortable exploring new sexual experiences.

Additionally, it's important to prioritize self-care and address any physical or mental health concerns that may be impacting your sexual experiences. Taking care of your overall health, including eating a healthy diet, getting regular exercise, and managing stress, can have a significant impact on your sexual pleasure and satisfaction.

In some cases, partners may struggle to find common ground in terms of sexual desires and preferences, in which case it may be helpful to seek out therapy or counseling to work through these challenges. Additionally, it's important to remember that sexual desires and preferences can change over time, and it's essential to continue checking in with each other and being open to making changes as needed.

In conclusion, enhancing sexual pleasure and satisfaction is a crucial aspect of creating a fulfilling and satisfying intimate life. Regular check-ins, open and honest communication, and a commitment to prioritizing self-care and addressing any challenges can help you build a stronger and more connected relationship.

Chapter 6: **Managing and overcoming sexual difficulties and dysfunctions**

Managing and Overcoming Sexual Difficulties and Dysfunctions

Sexual difficulties and dysfunctions are common and can have a negative impact on a person's quality of life. They can range from low libido to sexual pain, erectile dysfunction, and premature ejaculation. Fortunately, there are ways to manage and overcome these difficulties, and improve your sexual health and well-being.

1. Talk to a healthcare professional: The first step in overcoming sexual difficulties and dysfunctions is to seek help from a healthcare professional. They can help diagnose the problem and recommend appropriate treatment options.

2. Lifestyle changes: Making changes to your lifestyle, such as quitting smoking, reducing alcohol consumption, and exercising regularly, can help improve sexual health and reduce the risk of sexual difficulties and dysfunctions.

3. Mind-body techniques: Mind-body techniques, such as mindfulness and meditation, can help manage stress and anxiety, which can contribute to sexual difficulties.

4. Communication: Open and honest communication with your partner can help improve intimacy and sexual satisfaction.

5. Seek therapy: Cognitive-behavioral therapy and sex therapy can help manage and overcome sexual difficulties and dysfunctions by

addressing the psychological and emotional aspects of the issue.

6. Medications and treatments: In some cases, medications or treatments may be prescribed by a healthcare professional to address specific sexual difficulties and dysfunctions, such as erectile dysfunction or premature ejaculation.

7. Practice safe sex: Practicing safe sex can help reduce the risk of sexually transmitted infections (STIs), which can cause sexual difficulties and dysfunctions.

In conclusion, managing and overcoming sexual difficulties and dysfunctions requires a multi-faceted approach that includes seeking help from a healthcare professional, making lifestyle changes, using mind-body techniques, communicating openly with your partner, seeking therapy, and practicing safe sex. With the right support and care, it is possible to improve your sexual health and well-being.

Chapter 7: **Understanding and addressing sexual trauma and abuse**

Understanding and Addressing Sexual Trauma and Abuse

Sexual trauma and abuse can have a profound and lasting impact on a person's mental and physical health. It is important to understand and address this issue in order to support survivors and help them heal.

1. Definition: Sexual trauma and abuse refer to any non-consensual sexual experience, including sexual assault, rape, and childhood sexual abuse.

2. Symptoms: The effects of sexual trauma and abuse can be far-reaching

and include symptoms such as anxiety, depression, post-traumatic stress disorder (PTSD), sleep disturbances, and sexual difficulties.

3. Seeking help: It is important for survivors of sexual trauma and abuse to seek help as soon as possible. This may include talking to a trusted friend or family member, seeking medical care, or contacting a support organization.

4. Therapy: Therapy is an effective way for survivors of sexual trauma and abuse to process their experiences and work towards healing. Therapies such as cognitive-behavioral therapy (CBT) and eye movement desensitization and reprocessing (EMDR) have been shown to be particularly helpful for survivors.

5. Self-care: Engaging in self-care activities, such as exercise, mindfulness, and hobbies, can help survivors of sexual trauma and abuse manage their symptoms and improve their overall well-being.

6. Support: It is important for survivors of sexual trauma and abuse to have a support system, including friends and family members who are supportive and understanding. Joining a support group can also provide survivors with a sense of community and help them connect with others who have experienced similar experiences.

7. Legal action: Survivors of sexual trauma and abuse may choose to take legal action against their abuser. It is important for survivors to understand their rights and options for seeking justice and to know that they are not alone.

In conclusion, understanding and addressing sexual trauma and abuse is important for supporting survivors and helping them heal. This may include seeking help, therapy, self-care, support, and legal action. With the right support and care, survivors can work towards recovery and reclaim their lives.

Chapter 8: **Building intimacy and connection in sexual relationships**

Building Intimacy and Connection in Sexual Relationships

Intimacy and connection are important components of a healthy and satisfying sexual relationship. By building intimacy and connection, partners can deepen their bond and improve their sexual and emotional well-being.

1. Communication: Open and honest communication is key to building intimacy and connection in sexual relationships. Partners should talk about their desires, boundaries, and expectations to ensure that both parties feel comfortable and satisfied.

2. Trust: Trust is an essential ingredient in building intimacy and connection in

sexual relationships. Partners should work on building trust by being transparent and honest with each other, and by following through on commitments.

3. Emotional intimacy: Emotional intimacy involves sharing feelings, thoughts, and experiences with a partner. Partners can build emotional intimacy by spending time together, engaging in activities they both enjoy, and by being vulnerable and open with each other.

4. Physical intimacy: Physical intimacy, including sexual activity, is an important part of building intimacy and connection in sexual relationships. Partners should work to create a physical and emotional connection by being attentive to each other's needs and desires.

5. Shared experiences: Shared experiences, including new experiences and shared interests, can help build intimacy and connection in sexual relationships. Partners should work to create shared experiences and memories that deepen their bond and strengthen their relationship.

6. Quality time: Spending quality time together, including both alone time and time spent with others, can help build intimacy and connection in sexual relationships. Partners should prioritize spending time together and engage in activities that bring them closer.

7. Empathy: Empathy, or the ability to understand and share the feelings of another person, is an important aspect of building intimacy and connection in sexual relationships. Partners should work to cultivate empathy and

understanding by listening to each other, being supportive, and by putting themselves in each other's shoes.

In conclusion, building intimacy and connection in sexual relationships requires effort and commitment from both partners. This may involve open communication, trust, emotional and physical intimacy, shared experiences, quality time, and empathy. With the right ingredients, partners can build a strong and satisfying relationship that enriches their lives.

Chapter 9: **Navigating different sexual orientations and identities**

Navigating Different Sexual Orientations and Identities

Sexual orientation and identity are complex and personal aspects of one's life. It is important to understand and respect the diversity of sexual orientations and identities in order to create a supportive and inclusive environment.

1. Definition: Sexual orientation refers to a person's enduring pattern of emotional, romantic, and/or sexual attractions to others. Sexual identity refers to the individual's sense of self in relation to their sexual orientation.

2. Types of sexual orientations: There are many different sexual orientations, including heterosexual, homosexual,

bisexual, pansexual, asexual, and others.

3. Understanding: Understanding the different types of sexual orientations and identities is important for creating a supportive and inclusive environment. This includes learning about the experiences and perspectives of individuals with different sexual orientations and identities.

4. Support: It is important for individuals with diverse sexual orientations and identities to have access to supportive communities and resources. This may include LGBTQ+ organizations, support groups, and resources for education and advocacy.

5. Coming out: Coming out refers to the process of acknowledging and disclosing one's sexual orientation or

identity to others. This process can be difficult and complex, and it is important for individuals to be supported and respected in their journey.

6. Respect: It is important to respect and affirm the sexual orientations and identities of others. This includes avoiding judgment, stereotypes, and discrimination, and promoting a culture of inclusion and acceptance.

7. Allyship: Allies are individuals who support and advocate for individuals with diverse sexual orientations and identities. Allyship can take many forms, including education, advocacy, and support.

In conclusion, navigating different sexual orientations and identities is important for creating a supportive and inclusive environment. This includes understanding the diversity of sexual orientations and identities, providing access to supportive resources, promoting respect and inclusion, and engaging in allyship. By valuing diversity and promoting acceptance, we can create a world where everyone can be their authentic selves.

Chapter 10: **Developing a positive and healthy self-image when it comes to sexuality**

Developing a Positive and Healthy Self-Image when it comes to Sexuality

Having a positive and healthy self-image when it comes to sexuality is important for overall well-being and sexual satisfaction. A positive self-image can help individuals feel confident and comfortable in their sexuality, and can enhance their sexual experiences.

1. Education: Education and knowledge about sexuality can help individuals develop a positive self-image when it comes to sexuality. This may include learning about anatomy, sexual health, and different sexual practices and preferences.

2. Body positivity: Body positivity involves accepting and appreciating

one's body, regardless of shape, size, or appearance. Practicing body positivity can help individuals feel more confident and comfortable in their sexuality.

3. Media literacy: It is important to be media literate and to understand the impact of media on our self-image and sexuality. This includes recognizing the unrealistic and often harmful standards that are often portrayed in media, and choosing media that is positive and affirming.

4. Healthy relationships: Being in healthy relationships can help individuals develop a positive self-image when it comes to sexuality. This may involve setting clear boundaries, practicing safe sex, and ensuring that all parties involved are comfortable and satisfied.

5. Personal exploration: Personal exploration, including self-pleasure and masturbation, can help individuals develop a positive self-image when it comes to sexuality. This may involve discovering one's own desires, preferences, and boundaries.

6. Acceptance: Accepting and embracing one's own sexuality, regardless of social norms or expectations, is important for developing a positive self-image when it comes to sexuality. This may involve rejecting societal and cultural messages that shame or stigmatize certain sexual practices or preferences.

7. Support: Support from friends, family, and mental health professionals can help individuals develop a positive self-image when it comes to sexuality. This may include seeking therapy,

talking with trusted friends and family, or connecting with supportive communities.

In conclusion, developing a positive and healthy self-image when it comes to sexuality is important for overall well-being and sexual satisfaction. This may involve education, body positivity, media literacy, healthy relationships, personal exploration, acceptance, and support. By valuing and affirming one's own sexuality, individuals can enhance their sexual experiences and improve their overall well-being.

Chapter 11: **Understanding and managing the impact of past experiences on current sexual relationships**

Understanding and Managing the Impact of Past Experiences on Current Sexual Relationships

Past experiences, including sexual trauma, abuse, and negative sexual experiences, can have a significant impact on an individual's current sexual relationships. Understanding and managing this impact is important for improving sexual satisfaction and overall well-being.

1. Definition: Sexual trauma refers to any type of sexual experience that is harmful or traumatic, including abuse, assault, and exploitation. Negative sexual experiences refer to

experiences that are unsatisfying, unpleasant, or disappointing.

2. Impact: The impact of past experiences on current sexual relationships can be significant, and may include feelings of anxiety, fear, or discomfort during sexual activities. These experiences may also affect sexual function, desire, and intimacy.

3. Processing: Processing past experiences, including seeking therapy or support, can help individuals manage the impact of past experiences on their current sexual relationships. This may involve talking about the experiences, identifying triggers, and learning coping strategies.

4. Communication: Effective communication with partners is important for managing the impact of past experiences on current sexual

relationships. This may involve discussing past experiences, setting boundaries, and ensuring that all parties involved are comfortable and satisfied.

5. Boundaries: Establishing clear boundaries and practicing consent is important for managing the impact of past experiences on current sexual relationships. This may involve setting physical, emotional, and sexual boundaries, and ensuring that all parties involved are comfortable and satisfied.

6. Trauma-informed care: Trauma-informed care involves a compassionate and non-judgmental approach to therapy and support that recognizes the impact of past experiences on current well-being. This may involve seeking therapy from a provider who specializes in treating

individuals with a history of sexual trauma.

7. Self-care: Self-care is important for managing the impact of past experiences on current sexual relationships. This may involve engaging in activities that promote relaxation, such as exercise, mindfulness, or spending time with loved ones.

In conclusion, understanding and managing the impact of past experiences on current sexual relationships is important for improving sexual satisfaction and overall well-being. This may involve processing past experiences, effective communication, establishing boundaries, trauma-informed care, and self-care. By taking steps to address the impact of past experiences, individuals can improve their current sexual relationships and enhance their overall well-being

Chapter 12: **Practical tips and exercises for mastering intimacy in sexual experiences**

Practical Tips and Exercises for Mastering Intimacy in Sexual Experiences

Intimacy is a crucial aspect of sexual experiences, and can greatly enhance the overall satisfaction and enjoyment of sexual activities. Here are some practical tips and exercises for mastering intimacy in sexual experiences.

1. Communication: Effective communication is key to intimacy in sexual experiences. This may involve discussing desires, boundaries, and preferences, and ensuring that all parties involved are comfortable and satisfied.

2. Trust: Building trust with a partner is essential for intimacy in sexual

experiences. This may involve being open and honest about one's own feelings and experiences, and being respectful of a partner's boundaries.

3. Mindfulness: Practicing mindfulness can help individuals focus on the present moment, and enhance their experience of intimacy in sexual experiences. This may involve paying attention to one's own body and sensations, as well as to a partner's reactions.

4. Touch exercises: Touch exercises, such as sensual touch or massage, can help individuals develop intimacy in sexual experiences. This may involve exploring different types of touch, and discovering what feels pleasurable and satisfying.

5. Eye contact: Making eye contact during sexual experiences can help

individuals enhance their experience of intimacy. This may involve looking into a partner's eyes and connecting with them on an emotional level.

6. Slow and intentional movements: Slow and intentional movements during sexual activities can help individuals experience greater intimacy. This may involve taking time to savor each moment, and focusing on the sensations and sensations of both partners.

7. Experimentation: Experimenting with different sexual activities and techniques can help individuals discover new and enjoyable ways of experiencing intimacy in sexual experiences. This may involve exploring different positions, techniques, and preferences.

In conclusion, intimacy is a crucial aspect of sexual experiences, and can greatly enhance the overall satisfaction and enjoyment of sexual activities. Practical tips and exercises for mastering intimacy include communication, trust, mindfulness, touch exercises, eye contact, slow and intentional movements, and experimentation. By taking steps to enhance intimacy in sexual experiences, individuals can improve their sexual relationships and overall well-being

www.ingramcontent.com/pod-product-compliance
Lightning Source LLC
Chambersburg PA
CBHW060920130726
48001CB00006B/2331